MW01388113

Fabulously Fifty
and
Reflecting It!

Discovering My Lovable Me

By Tamara Elizabeth
www.MOXIMIZE.ME

Copyright © 2010 by **Tamara Elizabeth**

All rights reserved by the author. No part of this publication may be reproduced, stored in a retrieval system or transmitted in any form or by any means electronic, mechanical, photocopying, recording or otherwise, without the prior written permission of the author.

To my coach, my Mastermind and above all my friend, Barb.
Thank you—you are always the rock to my paper.

Once upon a time, there was a girl who followed along in her journey, not really knowing who she was or where she was really going. She tended to dwell on the past and continually had problems forgiving those that had wronged her; most of all, she didn't how to forgive herself.

This girl could not bear to think or talk about being lovable. She had stopped dreaming and put those on the shelf, because all of her dreams were labelled as unimportant. She had trouble fitting into her family and she felt she didn't fit in anywhere on this planet. In fact, she always questioned whether she was on the right planet in this universe.

She searched for the father figure she never had in her own father and that culminated in her first marrying an older man that her family approved of and then marrying a man her family never accepted. She produced four amazing children who are the loves of her life. When the first marriage dissolved after twenty-three years, she searched again and found her Prince Charming. They married and lived happily ever after!

WRONG!

This girl discovered one day that her Prince Charming was still a frog, warts and all. These warts were embraced, as they were part of this life. However, when the warts become demons that took on a life of their own, her life changed drastically. She put herself through self-blame and took on these warts as her problem. Her fairy-tale life disintegrated right in front of her eyes. As her hopes and dreams fell, so did her self-esteem, until she had nowhere to go but up.

As in every fairy-tale, a fairy godmother comes to the rescue. She is not there in the story to Band-Aid the wrongs and the hurts, but to ask the pertinent questions to help this little girl look inwards and see the authentic lovable self she was born to be. With this knowledge as a battle instrument, she learned to battle those evil warts and strive to come out as a victor in this journey. She overcame these challenges in her story and set out to continue living as a fabulously lovable girl.

This is my story, a story of a woman who has discovered, through reflections, the truly fabulously lovable me; the authentic me I was born to be.

Today I am a confident, lovable courageous woman who realizes that fairy-tales don't always have the ending of children's books, but they can have the ending and continuation of what we truly want and believe.

This book is the result of hard work and perseverance on a self-love journey. It is the reflection of my life; from these reflections I have created a workbook for you, the reader, to assist you on your own journey to find the most authentic loveable you.

My reflections shared are not to place blame on anyone in my path, for I take responsibility for my reactions to every challenge I have come across in my life. I just want you to understand that I have walked in your shoes and have never given up. You can restart your life at any time you want and still succeed in whatever you desire. This is not always easy, but if it were, the journey wouldn't be quite as exciting. Easy is never fun, to quote my fabulously wonderful self-love coach.

So I invite you into my world and to reflect upon your world. Enjoy the journey; I promise you it will be the most fabulously wonderful ride of your life.

Courage Prayer – Mother Teresa

There is a light that beckons you forward and it comes from within you.
Embrace it.
Don't try to hide in the shadow of fear it casts behind you.
For if you are committed to finding the courage to live with an open heart
There is no greater way to love others, or to love yourself, than to fulfill your unique potential,
To express your unique greatness and to become the unique leader you have it within you to become.
Finding the courage to be a leader and touch the lives of others in ways that only you can do, is the most profound act of love, and service, and significance.
Dare to want more from your life and to dig deeper into yourself to experience its mystery, its richness, and its sacredness more fully.
For when you do so you will see with greater clarity just how universal we all are.
And sensing that we are all part of a bigger whole, you will come to know, perhaps for the first time, that your life is truly holy, and that it is not just your responsibility to honor the sacred within you, but your obligation.
This is the truth that speaks from my heart.
I invite you to open yours to receive it.
"Give the world the best you have, and it may never be enough;
Give the world the best you've got anyway."

Read this book and promise to give yourself the best you are meant to be!

– Tamara
Master Motivator of Women in Transition

I. Past Reflections; Seeing The Past For What It Was

Challenges from the Past – Overcome

Learning to accept and allow. I have learned to accept the life I have lived for the simple reason that without this road I have travelled, I wouldn't have grown into the person I am. The parents I was given, the friends I met, the intimate relationships I experienced, my children, my step-child, the people I have met: they have all affected who I am. The good, bad, and ugly are all important to the design of me. I have allowed all the influences in my life to have a place and be looked at as positives. They have all been given to me to learn from; I embrace each opportunity for if the situations had been different, so would I.

Learning to think and say only positive things. Positive thoughts and positive self-talk are important to keep me in the present, enabling me to carry forward. This takes practice as I grew up in a home of not very positive beliefs. I always thought I was bad, that everything was my fault, and that I couldn't measure up. So with perseverance and determination, I have worked tirelessly to put a positive spin in my thoughts and self-talk. It makes a huge difference in my everyday living.

Always remember I am very loveable. It is my birthright to be loveable. I was born with the inner being of putting myself first and doing only things that make me happy. By loving myself unconditionally, I can then love others.

Learning to forgive. I desire not to only forgive myself, but also others. I always apologised for everything I thought I did wrong in my life, but forgiving myself or someone else for doing those wrong things was never instilled in me. Without forgiveness, I cannot move forward on my journey. Forgiveness releases us to the present and then we can carry on into the future. I forgive myself and it feels extremely good.

Take criticism for what it is. Do not take the criticism of others towards you personally. It is not the loveable me they are criticising; it might be my actions or decisions or something else, but it is not me. So take their observations and learn the positives from them. Don't take their comments to heart because they are not the boss of you and have no determination on who you are. You are the only boss of yourself, so you are the only one to change "you." I now take criticism as a positive challenge and work with it in only way: take it, digest it, learn from it, and throw it away when finished.

I can only change myself, not others. I had to lose the need to control my environment. Because of my upbringing, I never had control of my life. It was completely run by my parents' do's and don'ts. That is not entirely a bad thing, but I was never able to express my desires or dreams for me. I joined the theatre because when I played a character, I was accepted for that character. I was finally accepted even though it was really the character I played that was accepted, not the person I was and am. I now realize that I have the courage to change the only thing I can: me! It feels good and liberating. I love it!

Positivity rules! I always beat myself up as a youngster when I disappointed the people around me. I never learned to take every negative my journey threw at me and see the positive lesson in it for me. Now I have, and life is so much nicer. I look forward to challenges and negative situations so

I can look for the positive lesson and strengthen my character by hurdling that challenge and moving on.

Love yourself like there is no one else, smile to light up the universe, and laugh until it hurts and then... laugh again.

Have patience on my journey. It takes a lifetime to live and learn all that you need to be the fabulously wonderful you. I have had to learn that patience is not only a virtue, it is also a must in my self-love journey. Nothing comes perfect the first time round and I have had to learn to forgive myself as this is all a process. Live and learn, and then live and learn again.

Finally, for now but not forever, I have had to learn that the abundance of the universe is there for me to embrace. I am learning how and loving it! I will continue to practice my right of embracing all the abundance the universe has to offer, utilizing it to make a most fabulously loveable "me".

"Opposition is a natural part of life. Just as we develop our physical muscles through overcoming opposition - such as lifting weights – we develop our character muscles by overcoming challenges and adversity."

– Stephen R. Covey

"To overcome difficulties is to experience the full delight of existence."

– Arthur Schopenhauer

Question:

What challenges from your past can you see you have overcome, or still need to, and how?

_____

_____

_____

_____

_____

_____

_____

_____

_____

_____

_____

_____

_____

_____

_____

_____

_____

_____

_____

RELATIONSHIP WITH NARCISSISM

I Spent My life looking for a father figure, but funnily enough, I married my mother's persona.

When I was a little girl, I was the apple of my father's eye. My mother's dislike of this fact wasn't apparent until my sixteenth birthday. My dad gave me a beautiful surprise party at the Raquel Club with all my closest friends and family. At that moment, I thought I truly had my Prince Charming of a father and he was going to protect me from the big world forever more.

That did not come to pass. As I grew older, my relationship with my mother became more volatile and my father backed away from sticking up for me more and more.

Finally, when I was nineteen, I had had enough and married the first man I thought could replace my father as my protector and save me from my relationship with my domineering mother.

It didn't take long to realize this man was also not to be my protector because he melted under my mother's spell immediately and I knew I was hooked.

After twenty-five years and four lovely children to be very proud of, my husband and I parted ways. We had grown out of our relationship to each other and it was time to move on.

Because I hadn't gone through the self-love growth that I have done now, I didn't know the boundaries I have for myself in future relationships, including the one with myself. So I jumped into the next relationship I found when I mistook the man once again to be my protector. This Prince Charming turned out to be as narcissistic as my mother. So as creepy as it sounds, I have spent my life looking to marry my father figure, but wound up at mid-life married to my mother's persona.

I didn't discover until now that I mistook my mother's insecurity and egoism (or narcissism) for hatred of me. Actually, she probably didn't give me not a second thought all my life because she was so focused on herself and her needs. Once I understood the narcissistic persona, I realized that those were her issues and I was not to wear them.

This helped me recognize the same traits in my current husband and helped me understand that the issues of an addict are theirs, not mine. This gave me the courage to change my life and form the boundaries that I have for future relationships, including my own.

Alcoholism and narcissism walk hand in hand. If only I knew then what I know now.

"Love doesn't die a natural death. Love has to be killed, either by neglect or narcissism. Those guilty of these two crimes of the heart always hide behind excuses convenient; too ashamed, lacking in integrity and courage to face the truth. To them, it is always something other than their own actions, desires and self-importance that dictate circumstances. For these people, so blind to truth, true love can never be fully experienced for they have never really given of themselves all that they are."

– Frank Salvato

"Narcissism and self-deception are survival mechanisms without which many of us might just jump off a bridge."

– Todd Solondz

Question:

How have you handled the narcissistic person in your life?

_____

_____

_____

_____

_____

_____

_____

_____

_____

_____

_____

_____

_____

_____

_____

_____

_____

THE DAUGHTER OF A NARCISSIST

I am the daughter of a narcissist, and I survived. I grew up with a mother whose whole existence was about HER. If I were to run into the street and get hit by a car, it would not be the shock that she might lose me that would have move her to anxious emotion, but the fact that her hair appointment or her general daily schedule would have been interrupted by this incident.

For my whole life, I never thought I was important enough to love and that if my mother's day was ruined, it was because of me. One thing about being a daughter of a narcissist is that you are always trying to find a way for that person to love you. Love from a narcissist is conditional at best, if it every really is possible for the narcissist to love anyone but themselves.

When I was about five years old, at my sister's christening, I climbed onto the metal frame swing set in my best Sunday church clothes and slipped off. I caught my left wrist on a bolt that was sticking out of the metal and ripped the skin open in a two-inch wound. I was so scared of what this would do to my mother's mood that I ran and hid under my bed, bleeding profusely over my best dress.

Once my mother realized I was missing from the festivities and she found me, she was so upset about how I ruined her party and just started yelling at me. My hand never did get stitched and to this day, the scar reminds me of how bad I was in my mom's eyes. Luckily today, with the extensive self-love coaching I participate in, I realize that I was not a bad person who set out to mess up my mother's moment; I was a little girl who had an accident. Today, I know I am a good person and that incident was my mother's problem, not mine. I don't wear it anymore.

Another incident was when I ran into a street to get my ball that had rolled down the driveway. I chased it without thinking of the dangers in the street and was almost hit by an oncoming car. Luckily, there was no impact as the car saw me in time and screeched to a halt. Instead of my mother running over, scooping me up and cuddling my fears out of me, and appreciating that I wasn't easily hurt, she stood at the side of the road and screamed at me for being a bad girl and how this incident could have concluded with her having to cancel her hair appointment. I didn't live this incident down for a long time.

I grew up always believing I wasn't a good girl because my actions always affected my mother's life. It took until my therapy and self-love coaching to understand the mind of a narcissistic person. My actions were just of a young girl and they had nothing to do with my mother's insecurities. A narcissistic person is engrossed in excessive love or admiration of oneself. It is a psychological condition characterized by self-preoccupation, lack of empathy, and unconscious deficits in their self-esteem.

I have now learned that those traits belong to the

narcissistic and not to me. So when I look back on those times, I can now see them as a positive point in my journey as they taught me a lot about narcissism and about me. The scars, both physical and psychological, now just remind me that I am who I am and I love myself for it.

"Nobody can be kinder than the narcissist while you react to life in his own terms"

– *Elizabeth Bowen*

Question:

Do you wear what others think of you? Do you have a narcissist in your life?

How do you handle their existence?

_____

_____

_____

_____

_____

_____

_____

_____

_____

_____

_____

_____

_____

_____

_____

_____

_____

_____

_____

_____

_____

_____

WHO IS GOD?

Raised with a structured religion, I attended church on a regular basis. In my mind, I thought God was a man who ruled the Earth. He was a kind and gentle soul who taught us right from wrong. He encouraged us to be the best people we could be, treating all others with love and consideration.

Okay, so naive me grew up and discovered that if God truly wanted good on this Earth, he really missed the mark. I started meeting great and not so great people along my motherhood journey. Man, some people's children. Early on, I questioned who God really was. If he wanted so much good in the world, why was there so much evil? And why did good people die young while not so nice people lived on and on?

A dozen years ago, when my closest friends died of breast cancer before the age of forty, I gave up on the concept of a structured God. I started to believe in the power of angels because this justified the loss of my friends for me. They left behind twelve motherless children. I had to find meaning; believing these wonderful women became guardian angels for others on this planet helped me to understand things better.

As I have grown, I have turned my belief in a God into belief in a source of the universe. Now that I am on this self-love journey, I have come to firmly understand who God is for me. I still respect what others believe and am glad they embrace their belief fully. It is everyone's right to fully immerse themselves in what makes them happy and whole.

My belief in God has evolved into the firm belief of myself. My god dwells within myself exactly the way I am. The East call it "wrong thinking" if a person believes that we are to act differently if we have God dwelling within us. God wants us to act exactly the way we are meant to be; not in a spiritual way that we think God would want us to act. My god accepts me as I was made within my natural character. I would be amiss to act any differently

I have learned in loving myself that I have had to make peace with what I have been given. If my god wanted me to be any other way, He would have made me that way. Finally, being comfortable with me and embracing this is a relief. And I love it!!

With this belief firmly in hand, I now work on the "me" I am; I have the strength to ignore what others want me to be. This strengthens my character and endorses all things that make me loveable. I love the God I have and I enjoy having my spirituality; it completes me.

You can tell the size of your God by looking at the size of your worry list. The longer your list, the smaller your God. ~Author
– Unknown

You found God? If nobody claims him in thirty days, he's yours!
– Author Unknown

Question:
Who is God to you? How does your god complete you?

_____

_____

_____

_____

_____

_____

_____

_____

_____

_____

_____

_____

_____

_____

_____

_____

_____

_____

_____

_____

_____

_____

THE TRUE POWER OF "NO"

HOW TO HANDLE CRITICISM

I lived my whole life with "no" being the first word out of the mouths of my superiors. In fact, most of us will agree that this was the case during our upbringings. Not very often was there an explanation for the "no".

When I started raising my kids, I decided to use common sense and logic to explain the reason for my "no" or criticism. I also tried to place the person I was directing the criticism into the analogy so they could really feel how I felt and why I was negative to the situation.

For example: If my kids left me their dirty dishes in the sink or their dirty laundry on the floor in front of the washer, I would try to have them imagine them in my shoes. Did they have to pick up after me? Did I leave my dirty clothes for them to pick up and wash? The answer of course was a sulky, "No!" So I asked them if they would like me to start doing that to them? And again they softly replied, with their heads bowed, "No!" So I then told them my feelings on being treated that way and explained I didn't like it and that I didn't want it to continue.

Putting my kids in my shoes and logically pointing out the problem solved many issues, one of which would be why I would be saying "no" to their actions from now on.

I had a hard time receiving criticism without feeling rejection or hurt. It wasn't until I worked on my self -love affirmations that I realized the criticism was directed at my actions and not at me personally. Once I realized that it was easier to take the criticism and learn from it rather than personalizing it, I grew very fast and I now look at criticism as a form of compliment. If I wasn't doing something that was worth a criticism, then I wasn't doing anything and that meant not growing.

I know I am a good person so if someone criticises something I do, I desire an explanation so that I can forgive myself and move on rather than dwell on the action and move out of the present and into the past, which is not healthy for growth in my journey.

Criticism comes easier than craftsmanship.

–Zeuxis

If you are not criticized, you may not be doing much.

– Donald H. Rumsfeld

Do what you feel in your heart to be right - for you'll be criticized anyway. You'll be damned if you do, and damned if you don't.

– Eleanor Roosevelt

Question:
How do you handle criticism?

_____

_____

_____

_____

_____

_____

_____

_____

_____

_____

_____

_____

_____

_____

_____

_____

_____

_____

_____

_____

THE ALIEN ARRIVED

My hair totally fell out in large gross clumps in the March of 2009 and that was a huge turning point in my life. After all, it's not every day that the mother ship comes for a visit and returns you in five days looking like a member of their alien sibling tribe. When I came to reality, I wasn't sure if a lobotomy was included also. But looking back, maybe that would have been a good idea.

My husband was having another round with his demon mistress named alcohol, and he decided to walk out and go to his mother's in Vancouver for some major stroking of his "little boy inside." At the time, I just didn't understand the control substance abuse had over its victim so of course, I blamed myself and worked myself into such a tizzy that the effect of this was hair loss.

After realizing that my immediate future was wearing a wig, my friend and I decided to hunt out a beauty. What did I want to be: blonde, dark, pageboy, Farrah Fawcett? One thing about losing your hair, after the trauma subsides, playing "who do you want to be" can be fun! Fun! Fun! As it turned out, being who I really was and wearing a color and style for the real me was the only route to go. And you know what? That was OK with me because I loved it. Really I did. That is until I started wearing it on a full-time basis. Although it was made of real hair, it was itchy, hot, and completely bothersome. Was that how I was going to live my life from now until my hair returned if it did? No. So off came the expensive "rat" and it has sat on the mannequin head in the top of the closet until this very day.

Why is hair loss so devastating to humankind? There is a deep psychological basis for the trauma, but basically it was found during the Holocaust, that those fortunate enough to be incarcerated immediately had their heads shaven. The reason was to rob a person of their hair immediately, which in turn reduced their self-esteem. All too often, regardless of culture, hair defines our identity. Look at the celebrities over the decades.

It is true! The process of hair falling out of your scalp in bunches is relative to your self -esteem index rising.

Although my wig is put away, it is not totally out of sight because I want it to remind me that I can't let the problems of others become mine, otherwise I wear their problems in me and the punishment is hair loss. One hell of a lesson, but in this journey, I needed to learn it – even if it was a little drastic. Thanks Mother Ship!

If we can really understand the problem, the answer will come out of it, because the answer is not separate from the problem.
– Jiddu Krishnamurti

Question:

How do you handle situations you can control?

_____

_____

_____

_____

_____

_____

_____

_____

_____

_____

_____

_____

_____

_____

_____

_____

_____

_____

_____

_____

_____

_____

_____

INNER BEAUTY

After I realized that real hair on a head that is not made of Styrofoam was itchy, hot, and cumbersome, I decided to take it off and wear it no longer. It was time to bring my inner beauty to the surface and let it shine through. After all, if I am going to lose my hair, which is so important to us woman, - then have a funky SHORT cut! So I buzzed what was left short, in fact I was pretty well bald. I gasped, no I screeched in the mirror at first look. I considered covering all mirrors with wrapping paper so they would look like birthday presents instead of windows to my superficial self. But who am I kidding, there is more to me than what is or what is not on my head; I'm actually lucky I was a C-section birth because my head had no ugly malformations to it –wheh!

With time, this whole new look grew on me. The only change I desired first was to color the grey out because leaving it grey accentuated the bald spots, and I could only take so much change; bald might be beautiful but patchy grey, well that was just another story – that only looks good on the female canine species.

I decided that next in order was to get my makeup done to match the short hair-do. I thought about trying to accentuate my sexy cheekbones or my luscious lips, anything to keep the focus off my head and onto my face. I settled on my eyes and accented their green and gold. My eyes have always been referred to as "sunflower eyes". They have also had their color described as "breen" – combination of green and brown. I smile and communicate through my eyes; just ask my kids, they know <u>the </u>look.

Beauty is how you feel inside, and it reflects in your eyes. It is not something physical. ~ Sophia Loren

Letting my inner beauty radiate so large that people didn't even notice my hair, or lack of it was extremely motivating. It was one of my steps to learning and embracing self-love. I focused on who I am in the present instead of who I was with hair and who I would be if I had hair again. I celebrated the inner beauty that was bursting forth. It is very liberating to stay in the present and embrace who and what you are.

Some people, no matter how old they get, never lose their beauty - they merely move it from their faces into their hearts.
– Martin Buxbaum

My self-love cup runneth over and I finally fill fulfilled. Yeah! The wrapping paper can be ripped of all polished surfaces forever! What power that feeling was and still is as I reflect on that time. When I finally said, "To hell with it, love me for the inner me that radiates from my eyes and my heart, not what's on my head." My perseverance and enthusiasm would shout this out to everyone who crosses my path. I am an inspiration for others - I truly loved myself for that!

Beauty is not in the face; beauty is a light in the heart.
– Kahlil Gibran

Question:

Are you at the stage of starting over?

Reflect on the stages in your life that led you to this point.

Write the positives you learned from each stage.

_____

_____

_____

_____

_____

_____

_____

_____

_____

_____

_____

_____

_____

_____

_____

_____

_____

_____

_____

_____

_____

_____

_____

_____

Changing Life's Path

"Now you can finally take that decision that puts an end to your hostile and unfavourable situation. Remember that it'll be enough for you to make the first step, the rest will come alone. Take this opportunity and correct, once and for all, everything that is not right around you." This was my Ching one day.

The words that caught me were: "First step." I had been working hard to get to those two words for many months with my self-love coach. The determination to grow strong and happy enough to have the guts to take the first steps in the right direction on my life's path was hard work, but extremely challenging, getting me pumped up to carry on.

Without giving it another thought, I left my town and headed to the city to find myself a lawyer to protect myself from the toxic relationship in my life. I decided to not only find a lawyer, but also a new place I could call home. I needed to distance myself from small-town gossip and memories. To start again, I had to concentrate on being the present me and not the person others including my partner wanted me to be.

My circumstances weren't going to change anytime soon, but my attitudes to those circumstances could change and did. I bravely got on with things. I eventually moved to the big city, put on my heels and grown up attitude, confidently walked, my dogs and got on with life. I have me, I love myself, I have forgiven myself, and I am succeeding. I am a survivor.

Those first steps are not always easy, but they are necessary for growth and evolvement. Just as a baby tries his first steps, after a couple of wobbles and falls, he gets the strength behind his legs and keeps on going. Then look out, he never wants to stop walking. Your "first steps" in your new life towards change are similar. Once you get the feel of it, there is no stopping you.

"A happy person is not a person in a certain set of circumstances, but rather a person with a certain set of attitudes"

– Hugh Downs

"Do not follow where the path may lead. Go instead where there is no path and leave a trail"

– Muriel Strode

Question:

Have you come upon a change in your life's path? Describe your "first steps".

_____

_____

_____

_____

_____

_____

_____

_____

_____

_____

_____

_____

_____

_____

_____

_____

_____

_____

_____

_____

STEPPING BACK TO OBSERVE DOES NOT MEAN DEFEAT!

"It is the right moment to step back and observe the situation from outside, in a quiet corner. Renouncing action does not mean defeat; it is a sign of great wisdom. Collate your strengths, you will evaluate events and will intervene at the right moment with great success." My Ching one day.

This was suggested to me by my psychiatrist last November; yes I admit it, I had to seek psychiatric help because my self-worth had plummeted to the point of almost no return. That was the first step to getting me here writing this book. My psychiatrist told me to step back and look at my situation as if I were an outsider. Then decide what my next step would be.

So when I was in Maui for my annual migration to sun and sand, I decided to distant myself from the relationship I was in. I watched my spouse, mother-in law, and stepson from afar. What I witnessed was like an out-of-body experience. I was watching a poorly behaved eleven-year–old, with no boundaries whatsoever, treat his father and grandmother with no respect and getting away from it. I witnessed my spouse ignore his son's behaviour and only yell at him when his amount of alcohol for the day eased his conscience enough for him to feel bothered by his son. Then I sat back and watched a grandmother and a mom not worry one bit about the state of her son and grandson as long as it didn't bother her time in the sun. She and her son had daily drink-a-thons on who could consume more rum and cokes.

While I watched this around me, I realised that this was not the life I wanted. Everyone in this scenario is a very decent person in their own right, but together, they create a horrendous situation. I knew deep down that this relationship was not going to work out, but I just wasn't ready to admit it. I still looked at things with a defeatist attitude. More work on my self -love needed to be accomplished before I would be strong enough to continue taking the next steps on my journey.

I have to admit that my conclusions made upon watching things from afar did disturb me, and it made me realize I was the only thing that could be changed, but it was very scary to think of all that it encompassed. All the changes in my "perfect life", just the thought gave me the jitters and a sick feeling in my stomach. I couldn't intervene and fix the problems that I witnessed without great peril to my self-esteem; if I had any left. I had to hold an intervention with myself. We decided that we had to change the relationship with ourselves and decide what we needed to do to put myself and my happiness first.

So onward and upward; it still took time to get from November to now, July, but again it doesn't matter how I got here, it's just important that I did.

*"Most of us can read the writing on the wall; we just assume
it's addressed to someone else."*

– Ivern Ball

Question:

**Have you tried to look at your situation from the
outside? What did you notice? What are you going to do
about it?**

_____

_____

_____

_____

_____

_____

_____

_____

_____

_____

_____

_____

_____

_____

_____

_____

_____

_____

_____

_____

_____

_____

STEPPING OUT OF YOUR COMFORT ZONE

Being accepted to "Cambridge Who's Who" was not the challenge, just having the guts to apply, thinking myself worthy to apply was the bottom line. I applied just as an exercise in how to handle rejection and used this application as a positive way of displaying my growth in embracing rejection along my journey.

I am not being pessimistic with the last statement, I just didn't think I had much chance of acceptance and I had always had a problem with rejection, BUT the new "me" was ready to handle it properly.

With the help of my self-love coach, I learned that rejection is not about me but my ideas, actions, or opinions. So rejection is actually a positive moment in my life because it gives me a chance to re-evaluate my actions, decisions, or ideas. With that opportunity, I am able to grow.

Stepping out of my comfort zone is not new to me, but in the past I did it with great trepidation and not nearly as much confidence as I do now.

In the 1990s while my kids were in elementary school, our district needed more schools because the population was growing faster than the buildings and government budgets were. But as with all bureaucracies, there was just never enough money for the promises. I got mad and decided to do something about it.

My girlfriend and I decided to lobby the government for the schools they promised, I just didn't know how in the forefront I was going to be. Now that was scary. Here I find myself standing in front of thousands of people challenging the government on why they were not living up to their campaign promises.

I spoke powerfully after spending hours and hours on the perfect speech, but thank God the podium was solid because my knees were shaking so bad that my fierceness in what I was demanding would have looked a little like the cowardly lion if anyone could actually see my nerves. While I spoke with articulation and authority, I was actually trying very hard to talk myself out of throwing up. It is so good that humans are not transparent; I mean really what would I have looked like?

Well, I finished that night and many others. I grew and strengthened with each experience. Finally, I gave up fighting the government and decided to just build the two schools myself, one brick at a time. As our group sold our sixty thousands brick at $1 each, the government gave in to the media pressure and gave the money that had been allocated to those schools to us. We won, or should I say the kids won.

Today, there is a wall with all those bricks in it built into the high school we so badly needed. It was hard to step out of my comfort zone, but the kids needed me too and so did the real me. I am stronger today for that experience and I love it!

A dream is your creative vision for your life in the future. You must break out of your current comfort zone and become comfortable with the unfamiliar and the unknown.

– Denis Waitley

Question:

What experience did you have stepping out of your comfort zone? How did you handle it then? And now?

_____

_____

_____

_____

_____

_____

_____

_____

_____

_____

_____

_____

_____

_____

_____

_____

_____

_____

_____

_____

_____

_____

_____

_____

_____

BEING FABULOUSLY FIFTY AND STARTING OVER?

Forty is the old age of youth; fifty the youth of old age.
– Victor Hugo

With Mr Hugo's words to go by, I have decided to start my new life from scratch. This time I have half a century of experience and memories to learn by. I have worked, played, succeeded, failed, retried, failed again, laughed, cried, made mistakes, apologized, loved, lost, won, and most of all, I have lived.

I worked hard for fifty years to find out what I wanted to be when I grow up, and now I find I am just in the infancy of a new era: old age. So now I get to do what I want and be who I am, who I really am.

Growing old is mandatory; growing up is optional.
– Chili Davis

I think back to my thirties and I realize how lucky I have been to go through the experiences, both good and bad, that I have gone through.

Do not regret growing older. It is a privilege denied to many.
– Author Unknown

I lost three very close friends of mine to breast cancer before they reached forty. This time in my life opened my eyes to many things. My devotion to spirituality bloomed and my quest in finding my purpose on this journey intensified.

My first marriage dissolved after twenty-three years in an amicable way, and from that I got the greatest joys of my life: my four children who I adore to the max. Then I set on the trip of a lifetime. I married my high-school sweetheart and continued on my road to growing up. But did I really? I did as much as I could on my own. My reading of self-growth books increased, I employed counselling, and I went to Sedona, Arizona, for a week of heath and spirituality therapy.

My trip to China gave me the biggest eye-opener to what direction I was to go. In China, I was free to be who I wanted to be because 1.3 billion people didn't give a damn if I wore make up or even if I wore matching socks. The feeling was invigorating. This feeling was so overwhelming that I knew I never wanted it to leave me.

I was reborn and when I returned to Canada, I was firmly dedicated to doing what I had to in order to become the person that felt the way I did in China 24/7.

It took time, but eventually I discovered Barbora Knobova, my self-love coach, and I have never looked back. I know what I want to be when I grow up and I know where I want to go

And I am here and I am me!

Age is an issue of mind over matter. If you don't mind, it doesn't matter.

– Mark Twain

Question:

Are you at the stage of starting over?

Reflect on the stages in your life that led you to this point.

Write the positives you learned from each stage.

_____

_____

_____

_____

_____

_____

_____

_____

_____

_____

_____

_____

_____

_____

_____

_____

_____

_____

_____

_____

_____

II. PRESENT REFLECTIONS: THE PRESENT LOVABLE SELF

PRINCE CHARMING AND THE DEMON

The little girl inside you kept looking for the perfect father who would protect her and tame her dominant mother. Now you know this little girl is your ego, not your true self. Now you know that you're able to save yourself if you want to be saved.

What makes a "Prince Charming"? He'll be there for you always, he'll take care of you under any circumstances, and you will always be the most beautiful woman in his eyes. He will make you laugh. You will be yourself with him, and no one else. Right now, you're your own Prince Charming and that's the most important thing. The rest will come naturally when the time is right.

When I found my high-school sweetheart after thirty years apart, I thought my knight in shining armour was here to save me. We hit it off like we were still teenagers, and my love for him and life only increased over time in our relationship. Everything was going just fine, in my opinion, when my new husband decided to take on a mistress called alcoholism. It bit him in the butt and he was hooked. My prince turned ugly and the time of my life became the nightmare of my life. I had only read about people living and struggling with addiction, but when you wade knee-deep in it, it is nothing like the words on paper; it is so much worse. Not only are you in the middle of a confusing and abusive relationship, but it is with someone you love with all your heart. You can't understand why you have been deceived like this, why you hurt so much, why the person you adore now treats you the way he does.

You can't believe this is your life. You can only hope that when you wake up, it is all over. Only you wake up every day to begin the trials again.

Finally, I had had enough and I sought out help. Either I was the crazy one or he was. When I found therapy, I realized quite quickly that the problems of an alcoholic are just that: their problems and not mine, as I was so easily led to believe. This took time and effort and a great deal of self-love to come to believe and desire a better life for myself; to know I am worthy of that no matter what. My happiness is always number one. I believe in me and I now trust myself to make the best decisions to put myself first.

I have also learned to forgive myself for my mistakes so I can move on into the future and walk my journey with strength, determination, and pride, no matter where it may lead me.

"Forgiveness is the fragrance the violet sheds on the heel that crushed it."

– Mark Twain

Question:

What steps have you taken to learn to forgive yourself?

_____

_____

_____

_____

_____

_____

_____

_____

_____

_____

_____

_____

_____

_____

_____

_____

_____

_____

_____

_____

_____

_____

_____

_____

_____

WHAT IS THE UNIVERSE TRYING TO SAY?

Finally, after completing eight weeks in my self-love program, I came to the place in my growth where I knew exactly what I want out of a relationship, no matter who it is with. Then the universe knocked and I questioned if I had attained that goal yet or not.

One night, I received a phone call out of the blue from a long-time friend and confidant. I met this friend years ago after I had parted from my first marriage. He was then the head of an international health fundraising organization and I was applying for the position. We hit it off right away and he became like a protective brother to me. He always looked out for my wellbeing; he was the regional director for an investment agency and I became his client. For all these years, we have had a very lovely friendship.

Now on this night in question when he phoned me, I sensed something was off. First of all his voice and manner was as if he was under the influence of alcohol. That would not be too worrisome if it hadn't been for the fact that he was a very long-standing recovering alcoholic.

This conversation kept taking a turn for the weird as he expressed his love for me, going beyond brotherhood and he wanted to protect and look after me now in this time of need for me. Wait a minute! Rewind the tape! My Prince Charming was finally arriving now? And after he had fallen off the wagon, and a week after he had left his wife too?

What the heck was the universe sending me? Actually, what message was I sending out to the universe?

I was so confused and almost speechless. Luckily, I had enough of a voice for me to politely tell my friend that I appreciated his offer, but at this time the only relationship I wanted to be in was with myself.

Can you imagine the nerve? I was so freaked.

Then in my session with Barb, she got me to see this bizarre situation for what it really was. A test!

A person who could very well have become husband number three appeared on my doorstep and all my growth helped me to stand my ground and decline without my conscious knowledge at all.

I passed my test and achieved my main goal in this journey, which was to develop strict boundaries on who I would have a relationship with in the future.

This friend will always be a friend, but nothing more. I have outgrown him and I love myself for that. Whooohooo!

Always be a first-rate version of yourself, instead of a second-rate version of somebody else.

– Judy Garland

To be nobody but yourself in a world which is doing its best, night and day, to make you everybody else means to fight the hardest battle which any human being can fight; and never stop fighting.

– E.E. Cummings

Questions:

How have your set boundaries for your relationships been tested?

_____

_____

_____

_____

_____

_____

_____

_____

_____

_____

_____

_____

_____

_____

_____

_____

_____

_____

_____

SAYING WHAT ONE DESIRES

I spoke up when I wasn't even asked. I actually wanted to help this young girl and spoke up, not waiting to be asked my opinion. Instead of getting all hot and agitated, rehearsing my words, and not concentrating on the conversation, stumbling over my words in my head to get them right so that I wouldn't humiliate myself, I just offered my opinion. It was rejected by the girl due to her lack of maturity and I was fine with that. I didn't feel anything but love because I was courageous enough to speak my mind in the effort to help another woman. I left her with the message that she was to do what was right for her, but to keep my words near her heart so she could lean on them.

This experience solidifies my belief that I am now a strong, creative woman. I am articulate and love to be in the company of others. I say what I want, when I want, and am willing to take responsibilities for my words. The demon of fear has no power here.

There was a time when I would never speak of anything unless I was 100% sure it wasn't going to be rejected. This hindered my growth in intelligence and robbed the people around me of the right to continue an intelligent discussion on my opinions. Now I take this right and enjoy the feedback on my opinions, which can be both stimulating and a valuable way to make lasting friendships if handled correctly.

So when the chance for you to state your opinion comes, take a deep breath, stand tall, and speak with strength. You will be surprised at the respect you attract. Many around you wish they had the self-confidence to do what you do and they will want to share a piece of your power.

"He who does not have the courage to speak up for his rights cannot earn the respect of others."

– Rene G. Torres

Be still when you have nothing to say; when genuine passion moves you, say what you've got to say, and say it hot.

-– D. H. Lawrence

Question:

Why is it important to share your opinions with other?

_____
_____
_____
_____
_____
_____
_____
_____
_____
_____
_____
_____
_____
_____
_____
_____
_____
_____
_____
_____
_____
_____
_____

HAVE YOU EVER CRIED IN PUBLIC?

This is a skill that I haven't practiced often, but I did get a chance one day to see what my skill level was.

After my pilgrimage to the big city to start my new adventure, my emotions and exhaustion got the better of me while I was doing my first grocery shopping at the nearby organic grocer.

The whole situation came over me like a wall of water breaking. I was just near the assorted olive bar when I started to tear up. Then gush up, and finally dissolve into a complete tearful meltdown.

Imagine walking through a grocer's and finding a woman completing sobbing in the middle of it? What would you do? How would you react? You'd be surprised at the response I got. I felt like I was on one of the hidden camera shows. People, young and old, stopped to stare openly, secretly, or just walked past with a disgusted brush off. Some tilted their heads one way and then the other way as if changing direction would answer their silent questions. Some even pretended to drop things so they could indiscreetly gawk at my sobbing without being caught. Couples shifted their eyes between each other and nodded over my way. There were even others who boldly pointed.

My years of photography training helped me to observe the public's reaction of me having my emotional breakdown and these observations took my concentration from my sorrow and focused it on the people around me. Once I realized what I was doing, my torrent of tears turned into gales of laughter. If someone hadn't already called 911 for the loony bin to come and get me, there really should have been a call by this point. Even my girlfriend, who was trying

to be supportive, slinked off to observe the extensive salad bar, giving me space to get a grip.

No one came over to ask if they could help, and when I look back on the situation—who really goes to a grocery store to cry? Maybe if this outburst had occurred on the street, I might have been consoled by a stranger, but obviously not in the middle of an organic grocery store. Come to think of it, crying is extremely organic.

After my "emotional spell", I continued to the check-out as if all that had just happened was a very normal human need. I just hope I don't find myself on home videos shows anytime soon. But if it occurs to you to do just what I did, you can confidently tell anyone who asks what you are doing, "I am pulling a Tamara, thank you very much."

The soul would have no rainbow had the eyes no tears.
– John Vance Cheney

Question:
Could you cry in public? If you have, how did you feel afterward?

_____
_____
_____
_____
_____
_____
_____
_____
_____
_____
_____
_____
_____
_____
_____
_____
_____
_____
_____
_____
_____
_____
_____
_____

Our Minds Are Precious – Nurture Them

OPEN THE CAGE
by M.J. Waldock,

Fear, it paralyzes us to the core.
Our central being becomes trapped
in anxiety and doubt.
Caged like the lion we peer through
the bars at the outside.
Frantically pacing to understand
our dilemma and find an answer.
Always reaching through the openings
Grasping at the chance to gain freedom.
Open the cage, please, and let me out.

One of the reasons we as women don't want to change our lives is because of the beast known as FEAR. If our self-confidence is low and our self-esteem is on the brink of dissolving completely, we allow that beast to rear its ugly head and control our existence.

Until I took the self-love coaching program, I was a great play toy of fear. I feared being homeless, penniless, lonely, alone, etc. if I didn't stay in the relationship I was in. I didn't have the confidence to realize I had never been these things before so why would I now?

I never would have been able to move back to the big city after twenty years if I had let fear lead me. I would never have been able to set the boundaries for my past relationship if I had let fear be my leader. I would not have had the perseverance to develop myself into the woman I am today if I had let fear be my master.

Fear is inevitable in our lives; our ego welcomes it

graciously, but what we do with the monster is in our control. We are its master, not the reverse, and we must treat it so.

I have learned that by loving myself, I have beaten the beast of FEAR into submission. The only thing I can have control over and change is ME. I walk past the caged animal of fear with the confidence to know I can just leave it behind. It is caged and cannot hurt me anymore.

"You gain strength, courage and confidence by every experience in which you really stop to look fear in the face. You must do the thing you think you cannot do."

– Eleanor Roosevelt

"Inaction breeds doubt and fear. Action breeds confidence and courage. If you want to conquer fear, do not sit home and think about it. Go out and get busy."

– Dale Carnegie

Question:

How have you let fear control you?

What is you self-love affirmation for keeping fear in its cage?

_____

_____

_____

_____

_____

_____

_____

_____

_____

_____

_____

_____

_____

_____

_____

_____

_____

_____

_____

_____

THE INNER CHILD NEEDING TO BE LOVED

"First of all, NOTHING is wrong with me. I have to stop referring to myself as, "I'm a mess," and, "Something's wrong with me." That is the first step to getting my inner child in check and balance. I need to reinforce in me that I am going through a tough and challenging time, but that's all it is. I am going to deal with it and move on."

So who exactly am I arguing with? Who is this inner child anyway?

Your inner child (or as I like to call her - the 'little bitch'), is the part of your brain that collects all the junk we are fed about ourselves and our environment as we grow up. We are born as we are meant to be: our inner being. But as we pass through our lives, the inner being gets swallowed by the mischief of the inner child. We all tend to give this 'little bitch' way too much voice when it's our inner being that should be given the megaphone.

As I grew up, my inner child was fed things like: "Little girls are to be seen and not heard." "Your opinions don't count." "Your dreams are unimportant." You probably can think of your own traits that derive from listening to your inner child. Letting the opinions and actions of others is fuel for your inner child's strength. Believing 100% that you are the best you are and you have the right to be happy will slap that little bitch back into submission and let your inner being shine through!

An example of disciplining my inner child happened not very long ago. I realized through my self-love journey that if I stopped referring to my husband as such and started living with the truth that he is my ex-husband, I would become stronger and not let his selfish ideas about me pull me down.

59

I wanted to get out of this and I don't want to go back to the old me. I have worked too hard to strengthen the true me.

I will not let my ex-husband's words and actions influence the way I feel about myself. I left my husband, who never respected me; I have moved on and I have become strong, I have started a new life in another city – Vancouver. I will not let my happiness depend on how my ex-husband treats me.

Wow! Putting my inner child in her place really does feel good. It takes practice and sometimes she takes charge, but generally I give her a little talking to and she goes back to her corner waiting for the bell.

I choose to be to be free, independent, and to love myself no matter what the circumstances. I choose self-love and strength over self-destruction and pain. I choose to no longer let anyone make me feel miserable, as I am in charge of my own feelings and reactions.

I take responsibility for this choice and for how I act.

I am fabulously delicious and I will not let anyone tell me I am not.

It's ever so much more satisfying to get into a blissful place and attract a blissful person and live blissfully hereafter than to be in a negative place and attract a negative partner and then try to get happy from that negative place.

– Abraham

Question:
How do you keep your inner child in control?

_____

_____

_____

_____

_____

_____

_____

_____

_____

_____

_____

_____

_____

_____

_____

_____

_____

_____

_____

_____

_____

_____

NEW YEAR'S RESOLUTIONS ARE MADE TO BE BROKEN!

January 2010. Resolutions are being bandied about like wine flowing at a Gala. Phooey, I say. I never make them because I have never found anything worth fretting over to keep.

That is until this year, the year I complete my first half of a century on this Earth; a milestone to most, but an accomplishment to me.

So to celebrate this achievement, I decided to make a resolution and stick to it. I had finally decided I needed to find out what I wanted to be when I grew up, and this was the year to explore it.

I had been told by so many that I had a gift of designing small spaces into functional living places. So if you walk like a duck and quack like a duck...

Thank goodness for the techno age. What better place to create your own business than on the web? "Brilliant," I said, "let's get started." OK, hurdle #1 to get over. So I got on Twitter and Facebook and researched what kind of mentor/web designer was out there to help me reach my dreams.

After a few tries, I found someone I could meld with; they get what is in your head to their designing hands. It is refreshing, to say the least, when your ideas take formation. I have done this with designing many types of living spaces, but website space?

I was like a kid at Christmas as I watched my idea take on an existence of its own. Every Small Space was born May 15th 2010. I was the proud parent of a true joy; my own achievement. This wasn't important to me because I had finished a resolution as much as it was an accomplishment I achieved at my age. This time of turmoil in my journey yet a baby was born. I couldn't be prouder of my website and all that it stands for: success, accomplishment, perseverance, creativity, and intelligence.

Year's end is neither an end nor a beginning but a going on,
with all the wisdom that experience can instil in us.

– Hal Borland

Question:

What is your resolution at this moment? What can you do to see it through?

_____

_____

_____

_____

_____

_____

_____

_____

_____

_____

_____

_____

_____

_____

_____

_____

_____

_____

_____

_____

_____

_____

_____

_____

LOOKING AT LIFE IN SIX WORDS

<u>My/Frog/Turned/Prince/Now/Croaked</u>

There is a very good writing exercise for budding writers to learn to get their topic out in a concise manner. Take your topic or idea in mind and express it in exactly six words.

So to date this is my life in six words. Seven years ago when I ran into my high-school sweetheart after thirty years apart, I thought I had found my prince. I had just come from a very mutual divorce from my first husband of twenty-three years that had evolved into mundane and unexciting. We parted company with a shake of hands and our four grown kids being the best accomplishment of the union.

Then when I came across my high-school sweetheart, it was love at first sight again. Time seemed to never have passed, although a lot of things had in our lives. We were engaged shortly after meeting and married a year later in the most beautiful place in the world – Santorini, Greece. My stepson lived with us full-time and life with my new family was fun, fulfilling, and so very happy.

After just two years, my husband decided to take on a mistress: alcoholism and addiction to prescription drugs. The last twenty months of our marriage before I couldn't take any more was awful. The disease gripped my prince by the jugular and would not let up on its grip. The abuse, mental and physical, started to take a toll on my own health and mental wellbeing. As with any narcissist, an addict only looks out for himself and will pass the blame for his addictions on to everyone else but themselves. So now I had to let his problems and addictions be his problems and not take them on to my shoulders. The only thing I can change is myself and no one else. It takes a great deal of courage to resign myself to this fact, but it is the healthiest way to live.

This was one of the hardest decisions to make in my life but I have to look after my wellbeing and continue to grow in the direction that is good for me. I have to keep boundaries intact and not let go of them, no matter what.

So at this time, my prince turned back into a frog and will remain there until he decides to change his life. I, on the other hand, am moving on. This relationship has taught me to place secure boundaries around any relationship I have in the future, even the one I have with myself. No addicts or recovering addicts allowed.

*"I don't know if I continue, even today, always liking myself.
But what I learned to do many years ago was to forgive myself.
It is very important for every human being to forgive herself or
himself because if you live, you will make mistakes- it is
inevitable. But once you do and you see the mistake, then you
forgive yourself and say, 'well, if I'd known better I'd have done
better,' that's all."*

–Maya Angelou

Question:

**What are the six words you would use to state your life
at the moment?**

**Have you developed a self-love affirmation to forgive
yourself and others?**

_____

_____

_____

_____

_____

_____

_____

_____

_____

_____

_____

_____

_____

_____

_____

_____

DISCOVERING YOUR PASSION

Everyone uses the word passion in a cavalier manner. But what is a passion? A passion is something you feel so deep that you experience warmth in the gut and as it warms you from the inside out, you get this uncontrollable bubbling of your blood, as if it's carbonated. The feeling is so intense; you can't imagine feeling any other way - ever!

A passion is defined as: the state of the mind when it is powerfully acted upon and influenced by something external to itself; the state of any particular faculty which, under such conditions, becomes extremely sensitive or uncontrollably excited; any emotion or sentiment (specifically, love or anger) in a state of abnormal or controlling activity; an extreme or inordinate desire; also, the capacity or susceptibility of being so affected; as, to be in a passion; the passions of love, hate, jealously, wrath, ambition, avarice, fear.

(I personally like my definition better.)

During my self-love journey, I had the opportunity to take a Passion Test. The point of this test was to read a series of famous quotations that would help me dig deep into my inner being, the true me; the person I was born to be without the little bitch inner child messing things up. By digging deep, I would find my authentic passions by self-reflection. I wanted to make sure I had several passions because to only have one would make the rest of my journey a little uneventful not experiencing more.

It is human nature to only remember things in your life you are passionate about. Reflect but never stay on that finest moment too long. A true passion is to be experienced, embraced, and then you move on so you can experience the next one.

To be passionate about something keeps me in the present and that is so important in the self-love journey in finding the authentic me. Dwelling in the past is perfect fuel for my inner child, and she is too much work in the past. Your past is over; you have to forgive the wrongs, learn from them, and move on.

I'll give you an example of a quote in the test so you can see how I answered.

"Only passions, great passions can elevate the soul to great things."

– Denis Diderot

<u>*My self-reflection:*</u>

A passion energizes me. When energized, I can accomplish anything. A passion comes from the depths of my soul. Fuelling it helps me to reach the stars.

The most important lesson I learned from taking this test is that I believe in myself deeply. I love my answers and embrace all they give me in knowledge about myself.

"Only passions, great passions can elevate the soul to great things."

– Denis Diderot

Question:

What are you passionate about? I mean really carbonated-blood passionate about?

How do you celebrate this passion?

_____

_____

_____

_____

_____

_____

_____

_____

_____

_____

_____

_____

_____

_____

_____

_____

_____

_____

_____

_____

_____

_____

_____

THE LEMON TREE

"If life deals you lemons, make lemonade."

–Proverb

This proverb was made famous by Dale Carnegie when he summed up life using it in his famous quote: *"If life gives you lemons, make lemonade," meaning that one should make the best of bad situations.*

After fleeing my bad relationship to go to the big city for some distance, I decided one day that as a cathartic therapy for my self-help, I would design a group to join called Tamara's Lemon Tree on Facebook. As head lemon squeezer, I would provide the shade of a tree with plenty of comfortable chairs. There would be cold water, sugar, and pitchers. All anyone had to bring for the visit was their own lemons.

For each us with a lemon, we can make our own version of lemonade. No recipe is denied. There is no lemonade too sweet or too tart. Each glass should be made with the care and development that will soothe each member, as the cold liquid lines their throat. Tamara's' Lemon Tree is just a forum or portal for others to find help and strength in confirming their self-love. Their issues are theirs and theirs alone. I am only there to provide an ear. I can only share what happened on my journey and hope they find solace while continuing on theirs.

I have learned through my self-love coaching that I cannot take on the problems of others, as they are their own, not mine. I can only change how I grow, travel, and learn from my journey, not the journeys of others. But I hope by sharing my experiences, in some small amount they will find strength to carry on. Giving up has no place in life. As they say, you can't win the race if you don't enter it.

The definition to my lemonade is the final mixture of strength, determination, perseverance, and patience to succeed through the toughest of challenges. Life is not a dress rehearsal; we don't get a chance to relive our mistakes and correct them. So learn from them and turn them into positive moments in our journey before moving on. Hold you head high and walk with confidence. Don't forget to forgive yourself for the mistakes you have made and for those that have done wrong by you so you can move on and continue to walk into your future.

There are always potholes in the road of life. I sometimes wish I invested in a gravel pit, then my potholes would always have fill available, but life is not like that, is it? So remember; it's not the load you carry, it's how you carry that load.

It never ceases to amaze me that life, without any warning can see just how much you were actually paying attention, and throw something at you that is totally out of left field, taking your breath away while threatening to overtake you!

– Elizabeth for XquisitLife

Question:
What is your recipe for lemonade?

_____

_____

_____

_____

_____

_____

_____

_____

_____

_____

_____

_____

_____

_____

_____

_____

_____

_____

_____

_____

_____

WILD WOMAN, WISE WOMAN – AN ENDANGERED SPECIES

"Within every woman there is a wild and natural creature, a powerful force, filled with good instincts, passionate creativity, and ageless knowing. Her name is Wild Woman but she is an endangered species.
Though the gifts of wildish nature come to us at birth, society's attempt to 'civilize' us into rigid roles has plundered this treasure and muffled the deep, life-giving messages of our souls."

– Clarissa Pinkola Estes

But also within every woman, there is a wise and intelligent mind with brilliant ideas, filled with love, compassion, and kindness, unselfish thought, and endless thinking. Her name is Wise Woman, but she too is an endangered species.

Bringing these two forces together creates a stronger force filled with love, laughter, and the need to reach out and help others less fortunate, thus making a difference to our world.

I recently went to a fundraising event that a group of women put on. I was thrilled to see an event filled with women whose self-love was so strong that the room reverberated with the energy of self-confidence. It was electrifying.

The power of the women's sisterhood was so strong that it really could move mountains. All my hard work with my self-love coaching was rewarded at this event as I could really take part with confidence that I never had before.

In the past, I would never consider going to an event by myself, let alone with a friend. I never had the confidence that my conversation skills were strong enough, I was not

75

attractive enough, and I had nothing to offer because of the lack of letters after my name. So I would decline the invite and continue on doing nothing to better myself.

Now, with head held high, I accept these opportunities to celebrate life with the sisterhood of good women and enjoy being in the middle of the buzzing of the Butterfly Effect – where the movement of one butterfly's wing is felt on the other side of a continent, as its energy is continued with the flap of another butterfly's wing.

By becoming a true Wild Woman, Wise Woman, I have learned the importance of asking. With a sisterhood to lean on, asking for something is my right, as it their right to decide to accept my request or not. This discovery is so important to my growth and self-love. It is a delicious feeling, so try it!

There is a special place in hell for women who do not help other women.

– Madeleine K. Albright

Question:

How do you feed the Wild Woman, Wise woman in you?

III. FUTURE REFLECTIONS; LOOKING INTO LIFE'S FUTURE PATH

DEAR UNIVERSE,

I stand naked before you, with the barriers and walls crumbling around me, exposing my true and fabulously loveable self.

When I first ventured on my self- love journey to get to this place, at this moment, to say all I have to say to you, I was at the lowest point of my life. What was left of my self-esteem would have barely registered on a Richter scale. My identity consisted of being someone's mother, wife, friend, housekeeper, nanny, laundry-mat, cook, etc. but I forgot to be me. I was so busy giving to others that I forgot to refill me.

I didn't know what self-love was and I had a very hard time even talking about what was loveable about me. I was in a very controlling, toxic relationship with someone who chose addiction over me. I had not been happy for the past twenty months and no matter how hard I worked on making my partner and his son happy, the worse I felt.

I ended up in therapy and on medication to keep my emotions in check. I worried what others thought and I couldn't handle criticism. Even compliments were hard for me to believe, because I based my whole self-worth on a man I thought loved me, but didn't and never would; I didn't believe in myself. I forgot to love myself, which I now know is my birthright, something I am entitled to.

I decided that prescription drugs weren't the answer for finding my inner being, and that was when I went on my search to find out what was. Self-love coaching has been a wonderful journey, one that I'm still on, and will continue on till my last breath in this life.

After six months, I am in a wonderful life today. I have strong self-esteem. I believe in myself and even list proudly all that makes me loveable. I have a set of boundaries and rules that I live by. I enjoy life and love each day no matter what it brings; it's just ALL good!

I have worked hard on my self- love journey

I have created my website: Every Small Space.

I feel very accomplished and successful.

I created MEdotINC,LLC.

I changed my name to Tamara Elizabeth.

I moved to Vancouver with my dogs.

I learned to love myself.

I learned to forgive myself.

I have truly found my "Joi de Vivre"

Dear Universe, I stand before you and make the following commitment to you in the weeks to come.

I will no longer regard challenges as negative and

something to fear. Challenges will be embraced by me, and I will learn the positives they bring along with them.

I will continue to work hard in my self-love studies as I have seen proof it works.

I promise to continue to forgive myself and others so that I can move on.

I will also stay in the present and enjoy every second of my life no matter what it puts on my plate.

And...

...I promise to always love myself!

"Love yourself—accept yourself—forgive yourself—and be good to yourself, because without you the rest of us are without a source of many wonderful things."

– Leo F. Buscaglia

Question:
Write you own "Dear Universe" letter.
What would you say about the past you, present you, and the future you?

_____
_____
_____
_____
_____
_____
_____
_____
_____
_____
_____
_____
_____
_____
_____
_____
_____
_____
_____
_____
_____
_____
_____
_____
_____

FUTURE DESIRES

Love does not consist in gazing at each other but looking outward together in the same direction.

– Antoine Saint-Exupery

This saying perfectly describes what I look forward to in a relationship one day. I desire to find a partner that loves me for me, not what I can be for them. I desire my partner to walk beside me not in front of me. I desire someone who appreciates my likes and dislikes without trying to be or do the same. Differences are good and should be embraced as it keeps the excitement fuelled. Having two sets of footprints side-by-side in the sand, not just one. I no longer want to be carried or to carry my new partner.

I vow never to let another person steal from me; whether it is my soul or my money. I also vow never to allow another person to pass their excuses for their addictions onto my shoulders. The only items my shoulders are to carry from now on are my Pashminas that I have collected from around the fashion centers of the world.

These boundaries are important to install and enforce. They let you keep control of your self-love and stop you from giving of yourself without refuelling, and they keep you healthy both physically and mentally.

I now trust myself completely and love myself unconditionally so there is room for a relationship of equal proportions, not one ounce more or less. Walking together in the same direction but with individuality celebrated is a very exciting and long-time coming experience that I look forward to sharing.

I also desire to always be strong and steadfast with my commitment to put myself and my happiness first and foremost over anything else. I am important to me and to me only. Everything else is secondary on this journey.

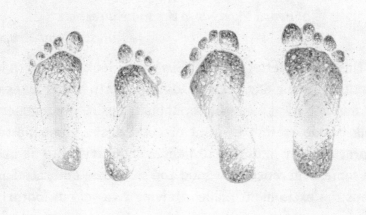

I desire the chance to embrace both the good times and the bad by looking at the bad in a whole different light. My Ching once said,

"Don't give up, even if something is worrying you. Make the most of this circumstance and transform every difficulty into a stimulus so that you can go ahead. Have faith in destiny which always changes bad into good. Luck is for the bravest!"

I have since then turned this into a life affirmation.

Dreams are renewable. No matter what our age or condition, there are still untapped possibilities within us and new beauty waiting to be born.

– Dr. Dale Turner

Question:
What are your future desires?

_____

_____

_____

_____

_____

_____

_____

_____

_____

_____

_____

_____

_____

_____

_____

_____

_____

_____

_____

_____

_____

_____

_____

IT ONLY TAKES A TINY STEP....

A TINY STEP

By M.J. Waldock
It only takes a tiny step
To cause a change
And have no regrets
First is the idea, for which toy
The fear and the doubt
Then the rush of joy
To laugh and cry
To Say Goodbye
To ideas that halt us so
Open your heart
To a day renewed
It is just the start
To a life that's yours
Forever

Thinking of the future is about beginning with each day and living in the moment. It is about starting the race because it is the only chance you have of finishing it; it is about loving yourself more than anything else and putting yourself above all else. It is about being so strong that the journey is exciting and thrilling, not fearful. Every mile brings good and bad, but always look at the bad as a lesson and learn from it; there really is never anything bad, just unpleasant for the moment. This brings the positivity out of every adventure and that is a good thing.

Tiny steps create confidence and you eventually accomplish the miles on the journey you are meant to travel.

No one counts the number of steps or the size of them in

your journey. Only you know what you have done to get where you are now. To learn to forgive yourself and build a new relationship with yourself is so important. Forgive yourself for tears, negative thoughts, forgetting to hug yourself, laugh at yourself, embrace your abundance, put yourself first, make your happiness the most important thing above all else and stop trying to control what you cannot control. Finally, change only what you can: you!

When I went to China, I will never forget that I, as a size eight shoe – which is average for North American women – was not able to buy any shoes because the average size for Chinese women is size five. After several frustrating moments trying to find shoes that fit, and feeling like a giant in the Lilliputian Land, a saleslady said to me in her broken English, "You come back when you size five." Well, we know that was never going to happen so I gave up on my addition of a pair of shoes to my collection from every country I have visited. The spot for China will remain empty. The point of this story is that no matter what shoe size you are, you can't change it; all you can do is keep on trucking in the size you have been given. You travel on this journey no matter what so only change what you can and go along with what you can't. Don't let anything halt your achievements and your dreams. Don't wait till you come back "size five", be proud of being "size eight" and keep moving forward.

Start wherever you are and start small.

– Rita Baily

Question:

What are your tiny steps going to be?

OTHERS CANNOT AFFECT YOUR FUTURE EXPERIENCES

Because others cannot vibrate in your experience, they cannot affect the outcome of your experience. They can hold their opinions, but unless their opinion affects your opinion, their opinion matters not at all. A million people could be pushing against you and it would not negatively affect you unless you push back. That million people pushing against you are affecting their millions of vibrations. They are affecting what happens in their experience. They are affecting their point of attraction, but it does not affect you unless you push against them.

– Abraham

Six months ago, this quote from Abraham (actually I didn't even know who or what Abraham was then and now I read him religiously every day) would have sounded anything but plain English to me. Now I embrace and allow every word to envelop me.

I see this as a very important lesson I have learned on my self-love journey. This is so valuable; all the hard work I have put into this portion of my journey would be wasted if I didn't learn to let what others think be just that – what others think, plain and simple.

I've looked at past intimate relationships, relationships with my kids, and the relationship with myself. I spent too many years letting the opinions of others affect my behaviour because I just didn't let them be: I pushed back.

You see, everyone has the right to their opinions. They have a right to have them heard, but that is where the rights end. Their opinions do not have the right to alter who you really are as a fabulously loveable person unless you let them. The opinions of others only affect their point of attraction, not you or I as we are truly meant to be.

This has been a hard lesson and one that I am still practicing because it is easier to let others affect us; that way we have excuses for our behaviour. But that is not taking responsibility for our actions and that is just as important as being and embracing who we are really meant to be.

This is taking destiny into our own hands. If we take control of ourselves and our behaviours, the future is ours to write. Destiny is defined by Webster as: The fixed order of things; invincible necessity; fate; a resistless power or agency conceived of as determining the future, whether in general or of an individual. So if I take control of my life, treat myself as the most important person in my life and constantly refill myself with self-love then I cannot fear my destiny for it is the natural order of things to come for me.

So don't give up the practice of letting the energies of others only positively affect you. Let all negatives be rebuffed and only attract positive people and actions. Make the most of all situations and circumstances. Transform every difficulty into a positive stimulus so you can go ahead. Have faith in destiny that always changes bad into good. And remember, luck is for the bravest!

It's choice - not chance - that determines your destiny.
– Jean Nidetch
There is no such thing as chance; and what seem to us merest
accident springs from the deepest source of destiny.
– Johann Friedrich Von Schiller

Question:
How do you ensure that you attract positive energy in your life?
What can you do to ensure your destiny?

_____
_____
_____
_____
_____
_____
_____
_____
_____
_____
_____
_____
_____
_____
_____
_____
_____
_____
_____

ECCENTRIC IN TRAINING

Traditionally the definition of eccentric is - ec·cen·tric :*adj.*
1. Departing from a recognized, conventional, or established norm or pattern.
2. odd; peculiar; strange; unusual
3. Deviating from a circular form or path, as in an elliptical orbit. n.
1. One that deviates markedly from an established norm, especially a person of odd or unconventional behaviour.

I like to define eccentric as someone who thinks outside of the box, looks at life differently than the majority of people. That is who I am becoming and I am enjoying the challenge.

Staying within the lines while crayoning makes for a very neat picture that society accepts on their wall, but I discovered that taking a chance to go outside the lines with color is acceptable to me and that is all that counts. It is my art and I am the only one who has to appreciate it. I do not have to base my like or dislike of this art on the opinions of others.

If being who you want to be is seen as eccentric by others, then be happy because your individuality is succeeding in showing through. The Bhagavad Gita – ancient Indian Yogic text – says that it is better to live your own destiny imperfectly than to live an imitation of someone else's life in perfection.

The Yogis also believe that we as a species are lucky to be humans. Human life is a very special opportunity because only in human form and mind can spiritual realization ever occur. For instance, turnips, spiders, coral, rabbits, etc. never get a chance to find out who they really are, but we do.

So we have the responsibility of searching for who we are. We cannot waste this valuable opportunity. Forget what others think, stay in the present and embrace who you are - eccentric or not - that's the best formula for a fabulous self-loving life.

As I get older, I am embracing my thoughts that fall outside the box. I find it exciting to be different and let the adventurer in me take charge. Every day, I am getting stronger against what others think of me. I try to turn it around and look at it that if they take the time to express an opinion about me, then I must be worth their time. So I will honour it!

Do not fear to be eccentric in opinion, for every opinion now accepted was once eccentric.

– Bertrand Russell

Eccentric doesn't bother me. 'Eccentric' being a poetic interpretation of a mathematical term meaning something that doesn't follow the lines - that's okay.

– Crispin Glover

Question:

What are your eccentricities? How can you enhance them?

_____

_____

_____

_____

_____

_____

_____

_____

_____

_____

_____

_____

_____

_____

_____

_____

_____

_____

_____

_____

MANIFESTING ABUNDANCE

The Universe is abundant with everything that you want. It's not testing you. It's benevolently providing for you. But you are the orchestrator. You are the definer, and you do it through your joyous anticipation. If there is an emotion that you want to foster, that would serve you very, very well, it is positive expectation. It is excited anticipation.

– Abraham

Manifesting abundance is something I finally realized I have the right to do regardless of who I am or where I come from. I deeply believe in what I desire and deserve; this manifests itself as abundance in my life. My every thought, whether I made it consciously or not, defines who I am. "You are what you think," has better odds than "you are what you eat."

Thoughts have power! So be careful how and what you think so your thoughts are manifested into a healthy, self-loveable you! The intensity and the quality of your thoughts also impact your life.

This statement isn't new; it actually all started the moment of birth and has continued ever since. While your thoughts may not have been of the highest quality when you were an infant, they were tools to help you understand the new world around you. Think about it, babies have the incredible power of manipulating the world around them so that it works in their favour.

Children are taught by their parents what to believe, and how to behave, thus moulding the perfect inner child. I speak from experience; my parents' favourite lines were, "You are to be seen and not heard." And, "Don't say anything unless you know what you are talking about." It goes on, but my point is that your thoughts are guided by your parents and by manifesting them at that time, they carry on into your adulthood and then your life is guided by those thoughts.

In my family, I could be anything I wanted as long as it fell into the guidelines of my parents. Lawyer, teacher, nurse... but whatever you do, don't want to be a psychologist, photographer, astronaut, computer wiz... those dreams didn't have a place in my household. It was far better that I forgot about my dreams of grandeur and abundance... forget the things that mattered most to me and do what I could do just to meet what was expected of me.

I know I can have an abundant life without relying solely on luck, and I don't have to always live a life of boredom, or stuck working at a job I can't stand, or even stay in a toxic relationship. I can do well - I have the right to do well; in fact, I deserve to do well.

This universal law for attracting universal abundance applies to every individual person on this Earth. This law will manifest itself uniquely to who you are just as a musician is bound to certain musical laws, but creates his own unique sound and style within those laws.

Now that I know all this, I plan to produce an amazing recipe for attracting everything wonderful from now on. That's my deal with the universe.

"Do not let your fire go out, spark by irreplaceable spark, in the hopeless swamps of the approximate, the not quite, the not at all. Do not let the hero in your soul perish in lonely frustration for the life you deserved, but have never been able to reach. *Check your road and the nature of your battle. The world you desired can be won. It exists, it is real, it is possible, and it is yours.*

– Ayn Rand

Question:

What are five ways you can manifest your universal abundance?

_____

_____

_____

_____

_____

_____

_____

_____

_____

_____

_____

_____

_____

_____

_____

_____

_____

_____

_____

_____

INVESTMENT 101

No, this isn't a lecture in financial investment, although that is important; this is a lecture on investing in you.

I was asked, "Should I invest in myself?" I thought about this question for a while and realized it was one of the most important questions to ask myself. I have nothing but the future ahead of me on my journey. So investing in me is a very important process in moving forward.

I had to look inside myself and listen to my emotions, for my deep emotions don't tell me lies; eventually, my answers are revealed from these emotions. This requires a lot of digging, but it is truly worth it. As you improve digging with practice, your desire for investing in yourself blossoms greatly.

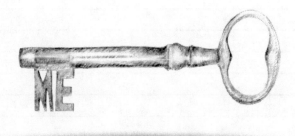

I have learned, embraced, and allowed myself to believe that I am the most important person in my life. I have to invest in myself. It is my right and my obligation to grant myself this. This is not selfishness. I need to take care of myself because I am the center of my life; I am the only one in my life who can changes things and make myself happy.

I believe I need to cater to my own needs if I want to be stronger. In order to support others and important causes I believe in, I must be stronger. Investing in me also affects my career, my family, my friends, and my world: my whole life. It is a glorious feeling, believe me!

The best investment in my life is in me. This means investing in love and generosity; in return I will attract my investment back in handfuls.

Once my chalice is full of investment in me, I can then afford to invest in others around me without compromising my purpose, my passion, or my vision. I believe in myself and my investment. I can't lose on this one for I am in control of my future.

So you ask, how am I planning to invest in me for the future? I have found what I want to be when I grow up, my niche: a self-love coach/mentor. My self-love journey has rolled out the red carpet and offered me the chance to be what I have yearned to be all along – I just didn't see it. I told my self–love coach I was so proud that my nineteen-year-old daughter was everything now I wished I could have been at her age. It was pointed out that I had been coaching all my life. My reward was helping develop a daughter full of self-esteem and self-direction. She truly loves herself and will settle for nothing that doesn't give her the best she deserves.

I am very proud of her and know that I can help others achieve their own success as I did with her and now myself. Finally, my chalice is full.

"If you want to be truly successful invest in yourself to get the knowledge you need to find your unique factor. When you find it and focus on it and persevere your success will blossom."

– Sidney Madwed

Question:

What grade will you achieve in Investment 101? How have you filled your chalice?

_____

_____

_____

_____

_____

_____

_____

_____

_____

_____

_____

_____

_____

_____

_____

_____

_____

_____

_____

_____

_____

WHY DO WE NEED RULES AND BOUNDARIES TO PROTECT OURSELVES?

The process of setting your boundaries and making your rules to protect yourself is a very large learning curve. Learning to stick to the rules you have set for yourself takes time in this school of life. Setting your rules and boundaries are just as hard for the person or relationship they are set against as they are for you to stick to.

An example: If you find the relationship you are in has deteriorated and you have moved on, but you still have some attachments to the past, you might want to set your rules with communication in the  future. Make your boundaries! No personal matters to be discussed. Only allow pre-organized phone calls and only emails dealing with the practical matters of the separation; all others are to be deleted. When your partner phones at a time not designated by you, you just ignore the call and text your partner back asking what the topic is. When you feel the fear of the possible conversation in the pit of your stomach, or the hair on the back of your neck rises,– listen to it and don't answer the call. Then YOU and only you decide when and if you wish to communicate. If harassing or hate email follows from the shunned partner, read the first sentence of the email, and then delete if it has no practical reason for being written.

When you break your rules, you will feel pain. It's kind of like breaking the law and going to jail. I have had my "Go Straight to Jail" card a couple of times, believe me. But you don't take it hard and blame yourself. Learn from the pain; it is teaching you how much you needed these rules. So write down these rules and say them over and over again. Embrace the experience and next time you will handle it better, or you won't because you haven't truly believed in them. So you will learn again and practice it again the next time your rules are challenged. This is a skill that you are practicing so don't beat yourself up about it. This will keep happening to you until you learn to absorb your rules. When you break them, you are to write them down and create affirmations so as to absorb the rules until they become a part of you without thinking, until it becomes like breathing.

Once you have broken your rule, forgive yourself and promise to stick to your rules in the future. This will make you stronger and you will continue to evolve into a better you.

Sometimes, "No" has to be so strong that there are many fences around it to make sure it stays, "No."

– Rebbetzin Chana Rachel Schusterman

Question:

What are your fences (rules) around your no to keep it no?

_____

_____

_____

_____

_____

_____

_____

_____

_____

_____

_____

_____

_____

_____

_____

_____

_____

_____

_____

_____

_____

_____

_____

BE THANKFUL!

I've mentioned keeping a Gratitude Journal many times during this book and I want to reinforce it in this chapter.

The first thing to do is just START a Gratitude Journal; or call it an Appreciation Journal. Choose a blank notebook or journal with a beautiful cover and pages. Something you would love to look at and write in every day; spoil yourself because you are worth every penny. Remember, it is going to be your trusted friend by your side for a very long time.

Then at the end of each day, take a few minutes to write five to ten things that you are grateful for that day. Make sure you look deep into yourself and really try to come up with five to ten different things to be grateful for each time you write. These things do not have to be big, even the smallest appreciation for something is important. For me some nights, it was just getting through the day without a hang-nail. I never wanted a day to go by without finding a purpose for it happening, because I cannot get that day back and the last thing I ever wanted to feel was those precious twenty-four hours were a waste.

Be thankful when you don't know something, for it gives you the opportunity to learn.

Be thankful for the difficult times. During those times you grow.

Be thankful for your limitations, because they give you opportunities for improvement.

Be thankful for your mistakes. They will teach you valuable lessons.

Be thankful when you're tired and weary, because it means you've made a difference

Be thankful that you don't already have everything you

desire. If you did, what would there be to look forward to?

Review your day and include anything that was a source of gratitude that day, however small or great, e.g., a baby's smile, a flower in bloom, the smell of a newly cut lawn, the sounds of the city, your quiet times, your hobbies, or your pets. Make the list very personal, add your favourite clippings, photos, quotes, or verses.

Write a few words about the benefits or blessings of that gratitude. Make what you write memorable so in times of stress you can go back and review your gratitude and really feel the emotions of your words. This is very powerful. Focus on the wonderful things in life to attract similar encounters in the course of the day. Use this newfound positive energy as a magnet to draw even more positive energy. Note these attractions in the gratitude journal. As more of your thoughts and words become positive, you'll start attracting more positive people and circumstances around you. Get into the habit of appreciating things. You'll be glad you did.

Remember that all gratitude doesn't need to be saved for the journal. Telling the people in your life how much you appreciate them gives as much to you as it does to them.

Their positive reactions rebound to put you in a positive mood too.

So tell anyone and everyone from your family to sales clerks and fellow employees that you encounter in your day how grateful you are to have them in your life; everyone likes to know they're appreciated. Watch your life evolve before you.

"God gave you a gift of 86,400 seconds today. Have you used one to say "thank you?"

– William A. Ward

Question:

Have you started your Grateful Journal? What are your ten things you are grateful for today?

_____

_____

_____

_____

_____

_____

_____

_____

_____

_____

_____

_____

_____

_____

_____

_____

_____

_____

_____

_____

_____

_____

_____

PUZZLE PIECES

I am not looking for the missing piece to my puzzle, because my puzzle has long been solved; I complete myself.

My giant puzzle is all in place for my future. It is a beautiful picture that took much time, forethought, and calculations to create.

The picture is painted with rolling hills, as a flat horizon would bore me too easily and now that I am used to learning and embracing my lessons of life, I don't want to stop now.

These hills will be covered with colourful wild flowers ever blooming and reseeding to bring new life every year. There will be lakes and waterfalls, as water is the very essence of life. And finally, there are silhouettes of two people walking hand-in-hand, facing the same direction, walking into the future, carrying on life's journey together.

My past relationships are not considered failures by me anymore because I have learned a few important facts.

We fall in love with people, but big deal. These men touched a place in my heart deeper than I thought possible, but it was only for a short term. Each relationship we experience is there in our journey to teach us something about the relationships and ourselves. I believe I have only tasted love.

I thought I found my soul mate with my last relationship; after all I have known and loved him since I was a young girl. It was a fairytale romance, but that is where the fairytale ended. Many of us misunderstand a soul mate as our perfect fit: the ying with the yang.

In fact, a soul mate is a mirror that shows you everything you are holding on to. This mirror brought me to my own attention so I could change my life in the present. This past relationship showed me everything that was holding me back from being who I really am.

To meet your soul mate is the most profound thing that could happen to you. This mate smacks you and tears down the brick walls you have so meticulously built around yourself. They come and do their job, and then thankfully they leave because if they stayed, the damage would be too great for you to recover from.

My problem was letting go. I still love this person; I just can't spend any more time with him. He came into my life to break open my heart so I could let my spiritual light in, and then move on to change my life. Once I finally realized this relationship had a very short shelf-life and moved on, I would be miserable. So I had to pick up my bootstraps and take this relationship for what it was. Now, again, I can take another first step and live the picture my completed puzzle shows and be happy.

"All persons are puzzles until at last we find in some word or act the key to the man, to the woman; straightway all their past words and actions lie in light before us."
– *Ralph Waldo Emerson*

Question:

Is your puzzle complete?

What does your picture look like?

If all pieces are not in place, what can you do to complete your puzzle picture?

_____
_____
_____
_____
_____
_____
_____
_____
_____
_____
_____
_____
_____
_____
_____
_____
_____
_____
_____
_____
_____

SELF-LOVE HAS A DEFINITE PLACE - NOW AND IN THE FUTURE

"Fabulously passionately loveable me – I am the best there is." My affirmation.

We have come to believe things about ourselves by what others think of us. We pick our beliefs and once we choose the ones that serve us as who we truly are and love ourselves for these beliefs, then self-love will abound. None of the beliefs we were surrounded with when growing up, either by parents or friends, were bad things. These people around us instilled in us the best beliefs they had to give us at that time to work with. We were taught to put everything around us first and our pleasures second. I know in my life my parents were first and foremost; making them happy with my actions was so important in our household. I put their happiness and being happy with me always paramount in my consciousness. My happiness and needs were always down the line or not thought of at all.

When I started my self-love journey, I didn't even understand let alone know what made me loveable. Now, after a great deal of work and perseverance, I can make a very long list of my loveable qualities. I am so happy to embrace this list and I love myself for this.

Self-love is who we are. It is our birthright and it is important to fulfill ourselves with all its glory. We feel so much better by loving ourselves than when we don't. We know it is important. In order to get what we want, we have to feel good, and to feel good, we must love ourselves. For vibrational alignment purposes, loving ourselves is everything.

I, along with millions of other people, grew up with no models for loving ourselves; how do we start if we don't have examples of unconditional self- love in our lives? My dogs give me great examples of it, but I know I need more than that. The more I consciously look for models of unconditional self-love, the easier it will become to find them and embrace their energy.

When I am hard on myself, I try to look at it by redirecting it through someone else, someone who is kind and good to me. I usually ask myself, "What would my mentor/coach say about this?" All I can say is pay attention to what you are feeling and redirect your feelings of love back toward yourself. This creates a very positive, strong energy aura around ourselves and that powerful energy attracts others with similar energy to us and together, we become a strong unit of universal power.

Be good to yourself in order to love yourself. Create a "very well-tended" vision for yourself. Look in the mirror and love what you see. There is no room for loving anyone else without loving yourself first. The vibrations you send out will not help those around you if those vibrations are not full of self-love. Vibrations attract vibrations.

Is self -love being selfishness? I know by now you are wondering where the line between self-love and being selfish is. When self-love is advocated, it is not suggesting we stop caring for others and just focus on ourselves. Being in service and giving back to your community is something that is very important to our self-image and success. Showing kindness to others and demonstrating our caring for our loved ones is key to having a fulfilling life. But to create a balance between what you give to others and what you give to yourself is critical. You cannot keep giving to others if you do not give to yourself first; remember the airplane spiel about the oxygen masks. Another example is when you pour water from a pitcher; ultimately it will empty unless you refill it. Like pouring water from a vessel, you cannot pour and pour without ever refilling it, it will eventually run dry. So we also need to refill, recharge, and re-energize. We need to replenish ourselves by loving and giving to ourselves.

Learning to love you may be the greatest love you ever experience and achieve. Self-love is not selfish or bad. Loving yourself will make you feel good about yourself, and in turn you will feel better about the world. This process will make it easier for you to give love to others. Embodying self-love will make you feel happier and you will attract much more pleasant people around you. This is also the best example we can set for everyone we encounter in our daily lives.

Having our self-love trained away by others around us is very common to almost everyone, but coming back to this natural state is easy as it is not hard to be who you really are. Loving yourself is a natural state of being, so give up all the excuses of why you can't and practice embracing your self-love. The more you believe it, the easy the wheels turn to filling yourself to the brim with love.

Love yourself first and everything else falls into line. You really have to love yourself to get anything done in this world.

– Lucille Ball

Love yourself unconditionally, just as you love those closest to you despite their faults.

– Les Brown

Question:

List the beliefs you were raised with about yourself. How can you turn these beliefs into positive components of your self-love?

_____

_____

_____

_____

_____

_____

_____

_____

_____

_____

_____

_____

_____

_____

_____

_____

_____

_____

Congratulations! You have finished this book and worksheets. You have successfully completed a small leg of your journey in discovering and living the fabulously lovable you. I encourage you to take action. Those actions are your God-given right to utilize because without action, you will always stay exactly where you are now or even before you took this book off the shelf and opened the cover and first few pages.

Look how far you have come in thirty chapters. Just picking up the book and working through it set you on a journey that doesn't end with the closing of the back cover. Continue the action you started and see where you will be in three months, six months, or in one year from now. You will be amazed that the feelings of triumph you are experiencing now will only intensify when exploring your self-love journey. You had to dig deep and reflect upon experiences that were wonderful and painful, I know, but you persevered and the rewards are bountiful. Keep the thoughts and ideas you wrote during your readings and look back upon them when times and challenges get tough. This will be a wonderful resource for years to come.

I want you to look towards your future through the four

E's of Empowerment as is your right to do:

Pursue your dreams and goal with **Enthusiasm**; the absorbing or controlling possession of the mind by any lively interest or pursuit.

Wake up each new day in your journey with **Excitement;** the state of being roused into action, or of having increased action; impulsion; agitation, and it is the excited state or condition.

Greet each new challenge along your journey with **Expectancy**; the condition of looking forward to something, especially with eagerness and anticipation.

But most of all live and embrace your fabulously lovable life with **Ecstasy**; a state of sudden, intense feeling and excessive, overmastering joy or enthusiasm. It is a state of emotion so intense that one is carried beyond rational thought and self-control.

I believe in you with the writing of this powerful book. Now it's your turn to believe in yourself by living each day with the four E's of Empowerment.

This book is just the tip of a fabulously wonderful adventure into self-loving. If you feel this taste of what a self-love journey can bring you has tantalized your taste buds for learning and experiencing more, then visit my website http://.................... And see what else there is in store for you to becoming the most fabulously wonderful person you have the right to be.

"Life's challenges are not supposed to paralyze you; they're supposed to help you discover who you are."- Bernice Johnson Reagon

Gratitude

"In the end, though, maybe we must all give up trying to payback the people in this world who sustain our lives. In the end, maybe it's wiser to surrender before the miraculous scope of human generosity and just to keep saying thank you, forever, and sincerely, for as long as we have voices."

– Elizabeth Gilbert

Eat Pray Love

I wish to thank all those that helped me on this fabulously lovable journey of self-love and authentication:

First and foremost, everyone in my life who has crossed my journey and challenged me to be the person I am meant to be. For every relationship and the lessons learned from their fabulous experiences. For all the good and not so good times, I embrace their existence and am so happen they occurred.

To the four greatest achievements of my life: Houston, Holt, Hudson, and Halstyn. You have been by my side through it all and I look fondly at helping to coach you through your own journey's challenges.

To my little man: you know who you are and I hope you take the foundations I laid for you and grow into the big man you are meant to be.

To the Boyz, for their unconditional love and constant sleeping by my side while I wrote and edited. Buddy and

Jackson, I love you.

To the wonderful eccentric AC. You have given me the strength all my life to ask from the universe and utilize all that I attract. Your eccentricities are valued in my reflections for now and for ever.

To top off all gratitude is my valued and very rich connection to my self-love coach: Barbora Knobova. The universe entwined us in February of 2010 and we have been virtually inseparable since then. She is the paper to my rock, and her unending questions have led me to a place of deep understanding, peace, and self-love. Thank you, Barb, for now I truly love myself and I am not afraid to embrace it!

Now that I have written my gratitude page, it is time for you to start your Gratitude Journal, one page at a time, daily. See helpful instructions and tips on the next page.

TIME TO WRITE YOUR OWN GRATITUDE JOURNAL

A gratitude journal is exactly what it says: a daily journey or diary documenting the five to ten things you are grateful for.

Gratitude is defined as a feeling of thankful appreciation for favours or benefits received.

Get yourself a perfect journal. Pick one that you love; money is no expense because you are worth it. Then pick a pen, any pen that you just love the look and feel of. Something your fingers love to hold and write with.

If you prefer, there are online journal sites like http://www.butterbeehappy.com/

Start your journal with the following line – *Dear Loveable Self, today I am fabulously grateful for...*

Every day, write down five to ten things you are grateful for. These things or feelings could be as simple as being able to eat your breakfast in the morning, the smell of the rain, a walk in the park, or a coffee with a good friend. You can also be grateful for the house you live in, having a supportive partner and family that are always there for you, etc..

What's most important about staying committed to your gratitude journal is when things are not going smoothly. This is where gratitude is most important. Writing only positive things in your journal every day will get you into the habit of looking for only the positive things in your daily journey. When times get tough, you dig deeper into your experiences to find the positive. Every pile of negatives has positive needles in the stack. With practice and dedication, digging for these lovely needles gets easier to unearth.

Every day, be grateful for something. Tell someone in your life you are grateful for them. This is a powerful way to express gratitude and it feels good too. Express your gratitude with the most important part of your face: a smile. Remember, fewer muscles are used to form a frown than break into a smile.

So no matter how you wish to create your gratitude journal, begin right now:

Dear Loveable Self, today I am fabulously grateful for...

_____

_____

_____

_____

_____

_____

_____

_____

_____

_____

_____

_____

_____

_____

_____

_____

_____

_____

_____

_____

_____

_____

_____